Trinity

Why Everyone Should be Catholic

Edward Korczynski

En Route Books and Media, LLC
Saint Louis, MO

Make the time

En Route Books and Media, LLC
5705 Rhodes Avenue
St. Louis, MO 63109

Cover credit: "Holy Trinity" by El Greco,
oil on canvas (c. 1577-1579)

Copyright © 2025 Edward Korczynski

ISBN-13: 979-8-88870-371-7
Library of Congress Control Number: 2025942431

No part of this book may be reproduced, stored in a retrieval system, or transmitted in any form, or by any means, electronic, mechanical, photocopying, or otherwise, without the prior written permission of the author.

Table of Contents

Prelude 1

Chapter One: Noah 11

Chapter Two: Abraham 17

Chapter Three: Moses 23

Chapter Four: Jesus 27

Chapter Five: First—That Which Needs to be Said 33

Chapter Six: Division 51

Chapter Seven: Be a Catholic / Become a Catholic 91

The Last Word 111

Terminology 117

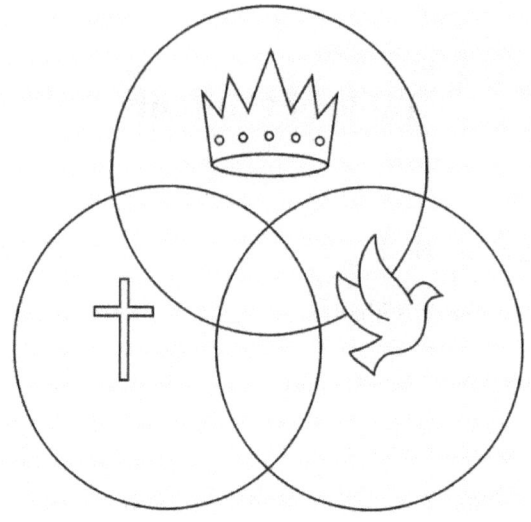

E. Margaret Korczynski

"Uneasy lies the head that wears the crown."
(Shakespeare, *Henry IV*, Part 2)

"Neither is there salvation in any other. For there is no other name under heaven given to men, whereby we must be saved." (Acts 4:12)

"For this is good and acceptable in the sight of God our Saviour, Who will have all men to be saved, and to come to the knowledge of the truth. For there is one God, and one mediator of God and men, the man Christ Jesus." (1 Timothy 2:3-5)

Prelude

It is a matter of either/or. You may question what I mean by that, and that is what this book will explore. Depending on who you are, your influences, and where you were raised, you will have a different association with the word Trinity. One might think of Trinity College in Cambridge, England, or perhaps Trinity College in Florida. The code name for the first nuclear test was Trinity, and that may be the association for some. The name Trinity, however, is Being itself: Father, Son, and Holy Ghost. For Catholics and most Christians, it is the only meaning of that word. We proclaim it when we bless ourselves. It is the answer to the question "Why is there something rather than nothing?" There is only one possible answer: God. I contend there is a method by which one can be sure of this fact. In order to argue that fact convincingly, we must begin by taking a step back to explore how God operates in His creation. Consequently, we must explore the case for and against Abraham, Moses, and Jesus; which is to say the case for and against religion and God. It is an either/or proposition, with no room for ambiguity or recusal.

God as Trinity is a mystery we do not fully comprehend. To clarify thinking about how there are three persons but only one God, the analogy with water is useful. All analogies limp, as does this one, but it provides some clarity. Water can exist in three different forms, and for this topic, we shall say three distinct persons: solid, liquid, and gas. All three forms are distinct, but all are water. In much the same way the Trinity consists of three distinct persons, but all are one in Being, God. With God, when one person is present, all are present. This may clarify how three persons are one God. It is one of the best analogies I have heard which attempts to illuminate the mystery of the Trinity.

Traveling to parts beyond, we will arrive at the one and only true religion. In the search for Truth, we will find God. Either the destination will result in our believing in God, in Jesus, the Son of God, the King of Kings, in the Holy Ghost, and in the Apostolic Catholic Church, or we will conclude with believing in nothing. I hope this volume will dissuade anyone from taking that disastrous and acataleptic route.

Allow me to continue the Prelude with a few existent conditions. Both Thomas Paine and Charles Dickens had observations about the times in which they lived; the former noted such were times to try men's souls, and the latter that the times were both the best and the worst. We share their sentiments because their observations accurately characterize our time. Therefore, there is great need for honor, devotion, and respect for Father, Son, and Holy Ghost throughout the universal Church. Then, through the Church, the Good News spreads across the earth. We are under attack. The attacks we are experiencing are coming from outside the Church as well as from within. They are not attacks merely on culture, art, beauty, justice, mercy, civility, reason, integrity, family, dignity, love, and a host of other aspects by which we conduct our lives. The attacks are on the foundational Being, God who underlies everything mentioned. These attacks are comprised of a prevalent attitude, which concentrates on local conditions and dismisses what is remote, assuming the remote has no effect on the local. With favorable conditions such as these, the attacks continue unimpeded.

Unfortunately, though not new, manipulation by outside forces is constant. The advances in technology have provided a means of new dominance. Currently, those manipulating have at their disposal tools of great power, ease of use, and sophistication. In part, those tools aided by other factors allow for the anesthetization of large segments of the population. It is occurring in the temporal realm and in the Church as well. This anesthesia is not a pharmaceutical drug, but it acts as one; it is the controlled dominating narrative. The cautionary tale about the emperor who had no clothes perfectly describes how it operates. Similar to the patient under anesthesia who is unaware of what is happening during an operation, large segments of the population are unaware of how they are manipulated, and in many cases, not even aware that it is occurring. I prefer to use the analogy of general anesthesia because it is more accurate than referring to large segments of the population as stupid. Moreover, I do not believe large segments are stupid; they may be ignorant. If one is sedated, it strips one of any control. If one is ignorant, it simply means information is missing about a particular subject of condition, etc. However, one can gain the information. The definition I use for stupid is an individual who refuses to accept reality as it exists; it is slipping into solipsism. For example, one may choose to believe the earth is flat. I prefer to think of those who hold this position as anesthetized, rather than stupid.

If you think I have overstated the concern, I am sure you know of, or have read of, attacks on one or more, or perhaps all of the aforementioned aspects. It may be helpful to provide a few examples. First a look at the temporal society and then at the Catholic Church.

It was not that long ago that friends, people I know, from all lifestyles (liberals, conservatives, theists, atheists, republicans, democrats, etc.) and I would have found it unimaginable that academia, business, and government would normalize the prevailing societal practices and find them acceptable. What are they? We can start with those, which are pure fabrication: a man transitioning into a woman, or a woman transitioning into a man, a transitioned man in a women's locker room, or bathroom, a transitioned man in a boxing ring fighting a woman, or any transitioned man competing against women in any sport. The next category is word play; definitions are changed, or substitutions provided. The definition of marriage has changed; no longer does it mean one woman and one man. Abortion, which is the murder of the unborn, is constantly referred to as women's health care. In public education, we have thousands of students graduating who cannot read, write, perform basic math, and know nothing about history, geography, or religion. In the political realm, government officials at all levels openly lie, and even when confronted and exposed are proud of their ability to be disingenuous. In broad general terms, there are government officials at every level who violate the laws of the United States by ignoring them. Prime examples are the border crisis and sanctuary cities. The people spoken of here are not stupid or ignorant; in fact, many of them are very intelligent and even brilliant. This is why I prefer to say they have been anesthetized.

In the civil or temporal order, we find all of this and more; however, the same is taking place in Christianity in general, and in Catholicism in particular. While there is much more to say about the civil order, I will turn to the Catholic Church; I turn to the Church because if there is to be a correction, it will have to come through the Church. It will not come from the civil order. When I was a child, I thought as a child; all was well in the world; all was well in the church; all was in the hands of God. As an adult, I know all is in the hands of God, and in addition, I know that not all is well in the world, nor is all well among the members of the Catholic Church. The Church, the bride of Christ, remains inviolable, but not so all of its members.

Evidentiary proof of the crisis and storm in the Church is substantial. It does not impugn or deny the great good the Church has done and continues to do. Neither is it an attack on Catholics or Christians in general. It points to what needs correction. Inducted into clergy and laity, influences from modernists, Masons, Protestants, and Judaism have spread error. Due to this, both the liturgy and the practice have changed dramatically. The change has not been positive. A sampling of some broad examples will follow below.

One of the most glaring problems is the shortage of priests and nuns, and the shortage of vocations. Feminism had a great deal to do with the problem concerning the nuns. With the priests, many factors are involved, and among them is the problem of homosexuality. The drop in the ranks of clergy and other religious, as well as the sexual problems, are issues the Church has not fully come to recognize or correct. As Pope Benedict XVI observed, we are headed towards a much smaller Church.

Another noticeable condition is the lack of formality. Examples of priests introducing extraneous and undignified elements into the mass, and the casual dress and atmosphere in many churches, indicates a decline toward the lowest common denominator. Sunday best, which was once a given, is now viewed as a retrograde attitude and dismissed by those who are supposedly of superior understanding. In the not too distant past, men used to attend professional baseball games dressed in suit and tie; now, in many churches we attend mass in flip flops, shorts and t-shirts. Why did we invert these priorities? What has caused us to fall into slumber? Have we all become somnambulists? Why do we take such a low road? One could shift the blame to poor catechetics on the part of the clergy, but before shifting the blame to the clergy, some introspective soul-searching is in order. The maintenance of one's faith certainly has the element of personal-responsibility. Before shifting blame to someone else, recall what St. Augustine had to say. Speaking about all of us, he said, we love truth when it enlightens; we hate it when it reproves. We love it when it reveals its own self and hate it when it reveals ourselves.

Messaging has also taken a turn for the worse. It seems we have demanded that we be welcomed, made happy by the music and comradery, never challenged, never confronted with difficult issues, and never made to feel uncomfortable. The clergy has been too willing to provide this and more. The voices who object to this kind of menu are ignored or ridiculed. Many of us find we are in a perplexing and frustrating position. We recognize a problem but are powerless to have it addressed in a meaningful way.

There has been a loss of the sacred and the beautiful. Both the visible arts and music have suffered from a poverty of beauty. There are exceptions, but they are exceptions: beauty and sacredness should be the norm, not the exception. Unrefined art and music have a place, but that place is not inside the House of God. We are all influenced or affected by these general conditions and fads. More will be explored as we continue in this volume. Keep your focus on the Father, Son, and Holy Ghost.

Chapter One

Noah

Initially, we must say a word about Noah. For most Christians, including Catholics, for members of other faiths and even for those who hold no particular religious faith, when Noah is mentioned the association that comes to mind is the flood. However, something much more momentous occurred at the same time, and many have overlooked it. After Adam and Eve are expelled from the garden, and the first murder occurs, humanity takes such an evil path that God contemplates eliminating all mankind. In some way, Noah finds grace before the Lord. The planned destruction is altered; God informs Noah a flood will engulf the entire earth and instructs him to build an ark. What happens next can be missed easily. God then does something of great importance for mankind; He establishes His covenant with Noah. Noah and his family will be saved, and it is through them that the earth will be repopulated. This first covenant with Noah is a covenant with all mankind. It is significant because it includes all the descendants of Noah: all mankind. It is the beginning of the second chance for mankind. With Noah, we have an incident of an either/or situation. Something extremely unusual in terms of some type of an encounter with God allowed Noah to know it was God and to follow His instructions. Noah did not question or doubt what he was told to do. He did so in an atmosphere where everyone around him believed him to be peculiar, eccentric, or oddly crazy. In chapter 6 of Genesis, verses 6 & 7 read as follows concerning God's mind,

> "It repented him that he had made man on the earth. And being touched inwardly with sorrow of heart, He said: I will destroy man, whom I have created, from the face of the earth, from man even to beast, from the creeping thing even to the fowls of the air, for it repenteth me that I have made them."

This revelation of the expression of God's mind is not an example of God's realizing He has made a mistake by creating man and the rest of life on earth. Rather, it is a revelation to man that evil has entered the world because of the fall, and that it should be avoided.

An encounter with God is no pedestrian experience. It must be an overwhelming experience causing one to question one's own state of mind. This either happened or it did not, and Moses, to whom is attributed the authorship of the first five books of the Bible, has recounted something authentic, or has created a fabulously false story. This is either a story for the childish and immature mind, or God's presence was so palpable that Noah knew it was God. In verse 8 of the same chapter, we are told that Noah found grace before the Lord. God called Noah just. The Bible does not give us details, but we can conclude that Noah had some knowledge or sense of the sacred. In some very significant ways, Noah was different from most of the men of his time. In some way, God was present even though the earth was corrupted, and Noah responded to that presence.

Did this happen or not? This is precisely the choice before each of us. It matters not if one is Christian, Jew, Muslim, some natural religion, or atheist, this remains for everyone the critical question. On it depends the fruitfulness of our lives on earth, and more importantly, in the life to come. As an aside, the existing atmosphere of evil at the time indicates we may not live in the worst of times, and certainly being surrounded by deception, confusion, manipulation, and evil is nothing new. God's plan will now move forward with Abraham, Moses, and His Son, Jesus.

REFLECTION: No. 1

For us 20th and now 21st century dwellers, Noah's extradictionary response and execution of God's directive would be unimaginable. At first blush, this tale about Noah appears to be a simple story about a flood and a man building an ark. Most people have that association when they hear the name Noah. On closer inspection, there are several striking and extremely important aspects to this story. As mentioned above, it is through Noah and his sons that the earth is repopulated. Noah's sons fail to follow their father's example, and God mercifully establishes another covenant with Abraham; salvation will come not through all of mankind, but through the descendants of Abraham. It is important to note that God's first covenant is with all of mankind, demonstrating God's love for all He has created. Noah's sons fall, as did Adam and Eve, and Satan before them. Through this second covenant, God will enter the world as a child born of a virgin. That virgin, Mary, is to become the mother of God. She, like Noah, did not fall; did not question; and did not doubt; she simply followed. The Israelites will now be the people through whom God sends His Son into the world, and it begins with the call of Abraham. From Abraham will come Israel and the Jewish people.

Chapter Two

Abraham

It seems we can hold Moses liable for quite a bit; accounts about Adam and Eve, Noah, Abraham, and himself. He is off the hook for Jesus. Well, perhaps that is a bit hasty to say since Moses also tells us about Melchisedech, the high priest, the King of Salem (Jerusalem), who offers bread and wine, and has no lineage. Melchisedech is extremely important and mysterious. There is scant reference to him and almost no information about him except that the mystery surrounding him suggests a very close resemblance to the WORD of God. He is a Priest and a King, and he has no lineage. The Old Testament, which is so very careful about providing lineages, is silent about this when it comes to Melchisedech. The scripture does not tell us from where he came or if he died.

We will begin this ride with Abram, his name before God changes it to Abraham. In that incident, God identifies Himself as *I Am* to Abraham. Abraham is called out of Ur of Chaldees in ancient Mesopotamia, in modern day southern Iraq. He travels to Haran, in modern day southeastern Turkey, and then travels with Lot south to Canaan, 400 miles away. Moses has given us a story, which is momentous. Abraham is a Semite, from whom will come both the Jews and the Muslims. Abraham was not a Jew or a Muslim; he was the progenitor of both Jews and Muslims.

When Abraham lived in Ur prior to his being called by God, he would have been surrounded by a society whose practices, such as human sacrifice, were repugnant to God. Human sacrifice would have taken a variety of forms. One of those forms would have been child sacrifice. We need to pause here for a comment.

REFLECTION: No. 2

Child sacrifice is alive and well. It is disturbing and, sad to say, a current practice in the United States and throughout the world. Abortion is child sacrifice; it is murder; and it is a holocaust. The statistics showing the number of abortions performed yearly throughout planet earth confirm that our enlightened, highly educated, and wealthy 21st century men and women have far exceeded the child sacrifice and murder totals of any civilization which has proceeded us. BMJ Global Health lists the number of abortions from 2015 to 2019 at 73 million. No reasonable human being can fail to recognize that the abortion holocaust dwarfs the numbers of any holocaust in history. In addition, if one rejects that, one is a true holocaust denier.

Unfortunately, there are Catholics, Catholic organizations, and catholic clergy and religious who support abortion. If you are a Catholic and support abortion, you are suffering from adiaphorism, which is the opinion that certain doctrines or practices in morals or religion are matters of indifference because they are neither commanded or forbidden in the Bible. This poses an enormous contradiction or disconnect. The question worth considering is, who among men has the authority and audacity to take the life of a person whom God, the creator of life, has decided to send into the world for a special purpose, a purpose known to none but God alone! It is evident the answer to this rhetorical question is that no one has the authority. The disparity we experience is amazing. Those who advocate for protecting a variety of animals, even insects, for eliminating of the death penalty for criminals, for protecting the water and air, and for decrying pollution are also the first to advocate for abortion. They either do not see the contradiction or choose to ignore it.

When God told Abraham to sacrifice his son, Isaac, Abraham would not have thought the request unusual. He would have known about, or even been present at, one of more of these types of sacrifices performed for placating the gods. It would have been common practice where he lived. What is striking is that Abraham is convinced that God has, in fact, contacted him. That contact, however it occurred, had to be extremely convincing. Perhaps Abraham was prepared ahead of time by God, not only for this request, but also for gradually becoming aware that God was being present to him. Scripture gives us no details, but Abraham does not question if it is God, nor does he question the command in any way. The scriptures do not elaborate about any misgivings or interior conflict he may have experienced. He sets out immediately to follow God's command without question. Noah, Abraham, and much later Mary are convinced it is God. The allicient nature of the call is what captivates each of them. These are all examples of the fact that God is present to humanity, never forcing, but allowing free choice in response to His urgings, as wonderfully exemplified by Noah, Abraham, and Mary.

With Abraham comes the next great covenant with the people chosen to bring the Word of God into the world for themselves, and through them to all of humanity. Scripture constantly reinforces the fact that despite the failure of men, God is constantly present and waiting for those whom He calls to respond to his call. Mankind constantly fails to live up to its part of the bargain; by contrast, God's mercy is tireless. It does not mean that God will simply overlook all our sins, both commissions and omissions: He will be a just judge. With the gift of free will comes personal responsibility, a requirement on our part, which through history we have attempted to sublimate.

Scripture portrays Abraham with all his warts. He lies, has several wives and concubines, but is willing to sacrifice his only son. That willingness speaks of a deep commitment to follow the will of God. It is a picture of the dilemma faced by all of us; will it be *Thy* will be done, or *my* will be done? Abraham's act of faith is rewarded, and eventually all of us are blessed because of it. The fact that he is not perfect displays the difficulty we all have in accepting the law of God, and the slow progress we make toward that goal. Noah's sons failed; thus, it is through Abraham, Isaac, and Jacob, who is renamed Israel, that the Messiah will come into the world. The Israelites will prosper for a time in Egypt, but are then enslaved and fall into idolatry. God comes to their rescue again; He sends them Moses to deliver them, instruct them in the law, and lead them to the Promised Land.

Chapter Three

Moses

We are all familiar with how Joseph, sold by his brothers, ends up in Egypt. Eventually, Joseph, his brothers, and that whole generation pass, and a new Pharaoh, who knows nothing of Joseph, takes command in Egypt. Thus, the stage for Moses is set. At mount Horeb or Sinai, Moses has an encounter with God; when Moses returns to Sinai he receives the commandments, and God reveals to Moses something He had not revealed to Abraham, Isaac, or Jacob: He reveals His name (Adonai) for the first time (Gen 6:3). Moses was His most faithful servant. God not only reveals His name to Moses, but also speaks directly with him (Numb 12: 5-8).

The story of Moses is well known; it is a story filled with miraculous works. For the first time, the Passover is celebrated, the priesthood is created, and the Israelites are given the law by which they are to conduct their lives. They are promised blessings if they obey the law and punishment if they disobey.

Moses provides specific examples of how they are to conduct their lives, and examples of what to avoid. The practices of the people who occupy the land promised to their ancestors are abhorrent to the Lord. The Israelites themselves are guilty of the same practices of the Egyptians. God begins the process of teaching the Israelites to abandon these very same practices. In the book of Leviticus, we read of the striking doctrine God gives to Moses. Enumerated are the specific prescriptions for behavior. They are all contained in two basic principles: be holy, because God is holy, and in all things practice justice—in other words love thy neighbor as thy self. To everyone at the time, including the Israelites, these had to be stunning doctrines by which to live. It was indeed a call by God to begin a new way of life.

Because of the dramatic events described in the Book of Exodus, it is possible to overlook some of the more subtle but vital details contained in the book. On display in the story of Moses, we see God's mercy and His seriousness. He promises great blessings but holds everyone accountable for their actions. At one point, God sends an angel to kill

Chapter Three: Moses

Moses because Moses has neglected to circumcise his son, Gresham. Sephora immediately circumcises Gresham and saves Moses's life. This event occurs when Moses, obedient to God, is on his way back to Egypt. It is a clear example of God expecting that humans must choose the good. Choosing evil results in chastisement from God.

Even when God chooses not to chastise, evil choices have their own resultant natural disastrous consequences. At one point, while in the desert of Sinai, God commands Moses to speak to a rock for it to bring forth water, yet he doubts, and instead strikes the rock with his staff. Because he doubted, God punishes him: he is not permitted to enter the Promised Land. It appears to be a very harsh punishment for such a faithful servant. Again, this is an example of God expecting us to uphold our part of the bargain. However, the story of Moses does not end in the Pentateuch. Because of God's mercy, what is denied to Moses initially is given to him later, as revealed in the New Testament. Moses enters the Promised Land when he appears with Elias and Jesus at the Transfiguration. This group of three is extremely important. Moses represents the Law,

Elias the Prophets. Jesus, the Christ, and the Son of God is the fulfillment of both.

The Father through the Son and in union with the Holy Ghost establishes a Covenant with Noah, and then a Covenant with Abraham, and one with Moses. He then provides for them the Law by which to live and sends the prophets to guide them on their journey through life. Because of backsliding, none of this is enough, and the Father sends the Word into the world to redeem it. Jesus through the sacrifice of His life redeems all of mankind. The gift of free will now enters the play; each of us will choose to follow Christ, the Messiah, the Son of God or not. That is the choice that determines our redemption. This brings us to the birth of Jesus. Through the Jews who follow Christ, and the early non-Jewish Christians, the word of God spreads throughout the entire earth.

Chapter Four

Jesus

God makes Himself known to the man Noah. He makes Himself known to the man Abraham, and to the man Moses. He then enters the world as a man to make himself known to all of mankind. Logos, Jesus, the Word of God, Christ the King – and although He is the King of Kings – He enters the world, like all earthly kings, as an infant. In contrast to every other king, His kingdom will never end because He is God. He does not have to enter the world as a conquering hero with an overwhelmingly powerful army of angels. He will conquer, not with brute force, but through the power of persuasion, through grace. He is born of a virgin, a small dependent babe who is destined to alter the course of human history. So much has been written about Jesus that there is nothing new I can add. I offer the following observations.

Overlooked by many is one of the most profound statements Jesus makes: "Think ye, that I am come to give peace on earth? I tell you; no; but separation" (Luke 12:51). In the gospel according to Matthew, we have: "Do not think that I came to send peace upon earth: I came not to send peace, but the sword" (Matthew 10:34). How often these passages are never addressed. The real Jesus is often ignored or white-washed to create a Jesus who conforms to our desires instead of our conforming ourselves to Him.

There is no denying that Jesus loves mankind and acts with great compassion, but ignored is the fact that He also makes demands. They are the same demands he gave to Moses in the burning bush. He simply states them again; it is the highest standard of behavior ever demanded of humanity: "Be you therefore perfect, as also your heavenly Father is perfect" (Matthew 5:48). It is a call to be worthy of God by working on the process of becoming a saint. Numerous saints and scholars have written so eloquently of Jesus that it leaves me only an opportunity to comment on the apostles.

Even the twelve apostles, who were the closest to Jesus of all His disciples, did not fully understand who He was until after the resurrection and the descent of the Holy Ghost on Pentecost. I base this observation partially on the following. When Jesus calms the wind and the sea and the apostles become frightened during the storm on the Sea of Galilee, the question they think to themselves is what manner of man is this? They still do not realize He was God in the flesh; they saw with their eyes a man, a very special man, indeed, but still a man. The apostles saw Jesus perform many miracles, yet they saw Him as a man who would rule an earthly kingdom, which would come about in their lifetimes.

When Jesus asks them "Who do you say I am?", Peter answers correctly. Even though Jesus confirms the answer was revealed to Peter by His Father in heaven, it becomes obvious later, that although Peter had the correct answer, he did not fully understand what it meant. He denies Christ three times. The apostles came to believe that Jesus was the promised messiah. They most probably believed He was the Son of God but did not fully understand what that meant. Most likely, as did many of the Jews of their day, they expected Jesus would provide a political solution to the Roman problem. They believed Jesus would be a ruling earthly king.

When the apostles were in the presence of Jesus after the resurrection, they questioned Him about the timing of when He would establish the kingdom in Israel. They believed He would rule and eliminate the Romans. When Christ was brought before the High Priest, and then Pilate, and subsequently crucified, the apostles' hope was obliterated. The man they thought was the messiah had been killed. They had to hide. They had been supporting a man whom the religious authorities considered anathema. They were alone, cut off from the Temple—outsiders in the Jewish society: they were traitors in the eyes of their fellow Jews. They had nowhere to go. The Romans would certainly not help them, and the Jews considered them outcasts.

When the apostles told Thomas they had seen the risen Lord, he refused to believe them unless he could see and touch the wounds of Jesus. It was only after they saw the risen Jesus and had the Holy Ghost descend upon them that they fully understood Jesus as God. John could then write the Logos was with God, and the Logos was God. John 16:16-22 is another example of the apostles not completely understanding exactly who Jesus was. It is not sur-

Chapter Four: Jesus

prising, then, considering the apostles who were in the presence of Jesus on a daily basis and still did not fully understand that he was the son of God, that many today, not seeing Jesus, have such difficulty in believing. There are many other examples in the scriptures that demonstrate that no one understood exactly who Jesus was until the resurrection.

One more example is in order because it is so telling. It comes from St. Luke's rendering of the Gospel. When His parents found 12-year-old Jesus in the Temple, Jesus questioned them as to why they did not know He was about His Father's business. Luke explains that Mary and Joseph did not understand what He said to them (Luke 2: 49-51). Here we have a clear indication that even Mary and Joseph, at that time, did not fully understand who Jesus was. None of this is surprising; in Jewish teaching and tradition, God was a spirit being, and God in human form was a foreign concept. The only examples of those who fully understand are the devils whom Jesus expels. They immediately recognize Him as the Son of God; they know exactly who He is. Jesus commands them to be silent; He will not allow them to disclose who He really is.

Why Jesus kept His identity hidden is explained in the parables. One of the demonstrable effects of the parables is to contrast power with mercy and power with goodness and beauty. This is precisely what Jesus is doing by keeping His identity hidden. He wants men to follow Him because of His goodness and holiness. In this way, they choose the good because they recognize it as good. If they knew He was all-powerful, they would follow out of fear. That is clearly the wrong motive. The resurrection and descent of the Holy Ghost changed everything. The frightened become the fearless, and the apostles begin to spread the gospel throughout the earth. We are the beneficiaries.

Chapter Five

First—That Which Needs to be Said

I would be remiss if I did not acknowledge the glaring fact that the Catholic Church is in a state of confusion and crisis. It is a fact that has been voiced by many in the clergy and laity. History assures us this is not a unique situation even though it may be new for many of us. Every age experiences some sort of crisis. The church hierarchy, led from 2013-2025 by Pope Francis, certainly made a mess, adding to the confusion and enabling the continuation of the current crisis. It created an amyctic atmosphere. There are issues on which the papal authority had been either ambiguous or outright contrary to the doctrines of Christ and the deposit of the faith. This caused great sorrow for many faithful Catholics. Some have been led astray and are in the unenviable situation of having become hollow men, practicing an empty faith. Others have left the Church, which is tragic for both them and the Church.

The estimated number of Catholics who left the Church in Germany alone in 2023 was 400,000. Some in the Church are pleased with the improvement over 2022. In that year, over 500,000 left the Church. Even more critical is the fact that Catholic attendance at mass, on a weekly basis, has fallen to dangerously low levels. These are facts which should not be ignored. They indicate a loss of faith, demonstrating that something has gone very wrong. In the face of such tragic developments, the Vatican was self-centered. It failed both to acknowledge the problem and to correct the trend.

If we are to evaluate by the fruits of their labor the job the leadership of the Church has done over the past sixty years, we might say they have failed miserably. However, we cannot just blame the Popes, cardinals, bishops, and priests; we, the laity are also guilty of neglecting the faith. We can perform a practical thought experiment. One may ask oneself: Who would continue to follow and refrain from questioning such incompetence in a business? Who would allow a sports team who was at the top in the standings to be decimated without a whimper? We laity have not been as assiduously mindful of our faith as we have been of our careers and our finances. In the past, as soon as the Vatican pronounced something, we simply complied. We failed to analyze and evaluate. We must accuse ourselves also. Jesus told us an evil tree will not produce good fruit, and a good tree will not produce evil fruit.

I am not suggesting that the hierarchy running the Church for the past sixty years has been and is now evil. That is for God to decide. I am considering actual results, which point to the fact that something has gone very wrong. Watering down the faith has had an abducent effect on the laity and clergy alike. In spite of the clear indication that the path forward must change, and in the face of all that has happened, the leadership of the Church has continued to either dumb down or violate the teaching of Christ and His Church. Cleverly cloaking their real aims, Pope Francis and other leaders issued statements or documents that appeared to be in line with traditional Catholic teaching. But they violated all of them in practice. The Pope accused traditionally-minded Catholics of creating division in the Church; however, he created that division.

I have selected a few issues to address. There are many, but I have selected the following because of the influence they have on the body of the Church: synodality, abortion, the TLM, the Eucharist revival, the stated position by Pope Francis and other clerics that hell is empty for all will be saved, and the excommunication of Archbishop Vigano. These issues are front and center on the minds of clergy and laity alike. My comments will be brief and to the point. There is a great deal of information published on these and other issues. Hopefully, you will explore each, consider all opinions, and exercise an informed mind to decide where you stand concerning them. It is sufficient to say all the issues deal with the traditions of the Church. They involve ignoring the deposit of the faith, watering down or altering the theology, and eliminating the beauty and majesty that has developed in the Church over the course of centuries.

We have a Church and faith that have made invaluable contributions to the development of Western culture. Without Christianity in general and Catholicism in particular, the arts, science, philosophy, notions of freedom, self-worth, ethical and moral

Chapter Five: First—That Which Needs to be Said

standards, politics, and all the other aspects of Western culture would not have come into existence as we know them. We begin with the selected topics below.

Synodality or the synodal process is vaguely understood by a vast number of clergy and laity. If, as it appears, synodality is a process by which the deposit of the faith is watered down, changed, or eliminated, and some new substitute takes its place, then it should be resisted and opposed. If, however, synodality means the exchange of ideas and collaboration between clergy and laity, this has been going on in the church since its beginning. It is a process that the current crop of clerics in the Vatican seems to believe they are the first to discover. In this, they make the error of the sixties generation which believed it had invented everything. If the first definition is the way the Vatican understands synodality, the process will produce enormous damage to clergy and laity. If the second, the Vatican need not to have done a thing. Not broken? Do not fix it. To an outside observer, as I am, the synodal process appears to be a Potemkin village where the participants' input is meaningless, and those who are steering and control the process have predetermined the conclusions.

The new "synodal church" along with the "new ecumenism," is a break from the Catholic Church. Together these two creations work as a "new proselytization." It is a proselytizing which is embraced by a significant number of the clergy in powerful positions. It is silently leading to a proselytization from Christianity to paganism. One of the surprising, disturbing, and devastating effects, accomplished by a methodical process, and by stealth, is to change the belief in the real presence of Christ in the Eucharist to one which sees it as a symbol. This, of course, is adopting the Protestant position. It appears that many in the clergy have concluded that Jesus did not mean what the Church has taught for the past two thousand years. They seem to believe that either Jesus got it wrong, or the Church got it wrong. Through a slow and patient process their intent is to change this belief, which they believe is in error. They have a huge blind spot, because the error is theirs. It is the repetition of the same error which led to the Protestant/Masonic distortion of the mass, the result of which is the Novus Ordo.

Chapter Five: First—That Which Needs to be Said

You may find yourself saying that what I have said is a wild, exaggerated accusation. If so, I suggest you check the number of churches where you find the Tabernacle in an inconspicuous or hidden place, where the Protestant method of receiving communion in the hand is practiced, where churches are full of laity who object to the installation of communion rails, and where Cardinal Cupich can write a letter advising the laity in his diocese not to kneel when receiving Holy Communion. The devil must be extremely pleased; he has the clergy and laity unknowingly destroying belief in the real presence while he relaxes. His work is being done for him by the very people who either do not recognize what they are doing, or do not believe in him to begin with. If some of the clergy and laity were intentionally attempting to destroy belief in the real presence, they could find no better way than what they are currently doing. They find themselves in the unenviable position of aiding the devil.

When it comes to abortion, except for a few exceptions, the laity has carried out most of the pro-life efforts. It is important for the laity to be heavily involved in this great work, but they could use the strong support of all the bishops, cardinals, priests, nuns, and the Vatican. Unfortunately, that has been lacking. If the laity had strong support from those quarters, through love, patience, and education, great strides could be made in the efforts to reduce and eliminate abortion. Pray that many in the hierarchy will stop being afraid to speak out and start acting according to the teaching of Christ. We have numerous examples of Catholics and other Christians being harassed or arrested even for silently praying at legal distances at abortion clinics. However, there is no practical response from the Vatican. I interpret such silence as sin by omission. I emphasize, this is not a judgment or condemnation; it is an observation.

E. Michael Jones has characterized abortion as a form of ethnic warfare. It is also religious warfare. When a Catholic or other Christian woman has an abortion, they become de-Christianized. For those who are Catholic, the confessional should be their next stop. For Protestants, a conversion is required. It is no secret that 82 Jewish Organizations expressed strong and unequivocal support for the Women's Health Protection Act, a name which is a misnomer. This kind of support is evidence of great confusion. Basing their reasons for supporting abortion on the Mishnah and the Babylonian Talmud, they have superseded the instructions given them by God, who loves them. They have managed to ignore both the Torah and Jeremiah. In the Torah, we have the 6th commandment, which is violated by abortion. In Jeremiah, we have the revelation that life in the womb is sacred. "Before I formed thee in the bowels of thy mother, I knew thee: and before thou camest forth out of the womb, I sanctified thee, and made thee a prophet unto the nations" (Jeremiah 1:5) The people who were privileged with this revelation have rejected it. Considering that God knows each of us even before we are formed in the womb, every argument in support of abortion is exposed as a lie.

Catholics can support, finance, condone, or otherwise aid the practice of abortion, but they may not do so. The ability to do something is one thing; the moral prohibition of doing it is quite another. Supporting abortion in any way places a Catholic in the state of mortal sin and in peril of spiritual death. In the Nazi concentration camps, hundreds of thousands of innocent people were murdered, and in the war millions of lives were lost. Among them were thousands of Catholic priests, nuns, and lay people. In fact, the first prisoners at Dachau were Catholic priests. The Jewish population of Europe was sent to the camps simply because they were Jewish. Priests, nuns, and other Catholics and Christians were sent to the camps for a similar reason, they were Christians. The regime dispatched anyone for any reason to the camps. Repression was the order of the day. All atheistic, totalitarian regimes believe only in the rules they create. Everyone must believe and adhere to their rules—except for them, they are exempt.

The profound tragedy of death in the camps and death by abortion lies not only in the fact that individual lives were extinguished. The termination of each life precludes the continuation of life. Each person whose life was and is stamped out (in the case of abortions, the killing continues) is deprived of children, grandchildren, and future generations. No human can rectify this tragedy. Jesus, the Son of God, can restore life and provide the blessings taken from those who were and continue to be murdered. "And think not to say within yourselves, We have

Abraham for our father. For I tell you that God is able of these stones to raise up children to Abraham" (Matthew 3:9). Since our Lord Jesus can raise children from stones, He can also correct every evil men have wrought. He is able to give life to those who lost their lives, and to give them children and grandchildren.

The TLM, the Traditional Latin Mass, is a treasure of beauty and sacred worship of God. It reflects the deposit of the faith passed on to us from Christ through the apostles and their successors. The effort to ban it is perverse, and we need to pray that the Holy Ghost will enlighten the minds and hearts, and open the eyes of those attempting this travesty. I attend the Latin Mass; when I have to attend a Novus Ordo mass the impression I have is that it is a superficial Protestant/Masonic concoction with little evidence that it is the sacrifice of Calvary we are attending. The service reminds me of the words Shakespeare placed in the mouth of Claudius: "My words fly up; my thoughts remain below." At the TLM, the opposite is true: the thoughts fly up; our words stay here below to spread the Gospel of Christ, Jesus. Consider how the Mass was changed.

Think of a piece of music or a popular Christmas carol or other song you know. After 1800 years of the melodic line and harmonic structure being passed down from generation to generation, the "experts" come along and change both the melody and harmony. No one would accept such a change because it would destroy the beauty of the piece of music and display enormous disrespect for the composer and those who preserved the music.

How was the sacredness of the TLM overturned so easily? As Catholics, we are familiar with "O Holy Night" by Adolphe Adam. Even those who do not sing know the melody and harmony of the piece. If the "experts" told the singers and musicians that they have altered the piece so that every third note would be one-half tone higher or lower, and that they changed every third or fourth chord to add more dissonance, the idea would have been rejected immediately. It would have been rejected because everyone would have recognized the intended destruction immediately. I ask again, why was there no outcry when the Holy Sacrifice of the Mass was distorted? The small group of laity and clergy who op-

Chapter Five: First—That Which Needs to be Said

posed the new mass were ridiculed and dispatched with alacrity.

I am not implying or saying members of the clergy who celebrate the Novus Ordo with sacredness or devout Catholics who attend the Novus Ordo attend an illegitimate service. My point is that it is deficient, open to much abuse in many places, and subject to endless tampering, which as it becomes normative, will lead to an empty faith. The service is spiritually still. If water remains still too long, it becomes stagnant. A liturgical service which remains still suffers the same fate. Like a white room, it is sterile. The Novus Ordo is disordered; it moved away from the order of the Traditional mass, which concentrates on the sacrificial nature of the Mass, to an endless variety of less than sacred innovations. This is not true in all Churches, but it is wide spread enough to cause confusion and damage. When I am asked why I believe the TLM is so sacred and beautiful, no answer is necessary or possible. The very fact that it has been asked indicates the questioner would not understand the answer.

The current Eucharistic revival can be a great success. Estimates are that 70% of Catholics do not believe in the real presence. Perhaps this number is correct, but it may not be. I would be upset if only 1% held that opinion. There can be success, but by following the current path, there will be none. The foolproof way of ensuring success in bringing Catholics to the knowledge that Christ is present in the Eucharist in every Catholic Church in the world would be to do the following: return the tabernacle to the center of the altar, arrange every altar so the mass is said Ad Orientem, install altar rails, and return to reception of Holy Communion only on the tongue. Use only sacred music for mass, preferably Gregorian chant. Use the TLM form of Holy Mass; in the U. S. have the laity procure missals with Latin and English text. Have the priests and altar boys, and altar boys only, no girls, recite the prayers aloud rather than under voiced or silently. Have scripture readings at Mass read only by the priest or deacon, and by only male deacons. Many Catholics will criticize me for these recommendations, and I am sure many of them will be in the clergy, but do this and not only will Catholics believe in the real presence, the problem of having empty churches will change into the need to build new churches.

Chapter Five: First—That Which Needs to be Said

"Hell is empty and all will be saved." This type of reflection most likely proceeds from the writings of Pierre Teilhard de Chardin. I am not qualified to comment on all the philosophical implications of Chardin's views. What is clear, however, is that one of Chardin's major themes is that all creation is moving toward perfection. This is a very heartwarming proposition; however, there is no evidence to support such an idea. Many biblical scholars say the evidence we do have indicates the opposite. This alone suggests that the case for hell being empty, and all being saved, is an idea to be discussed with great caution, and certainly not taught as fact. One can think of Chardin's notion of movement toward perfection from two very divergent and opposing perspectives.

Pope Francis and others in the hierarchy are known to have held one of those perspectives, as evidenced by documents issued by the Vatican. They espouse that all are saved, and this looks suspiciously like adopting the Protestant notion that individual behavior has no effect on the fact that we have been saved by Christ, Jesus. They appear to have dismissed the references Our Lord made to a just judgment. They have also ignored the fact that Jesus said if we love Him, we must keep His commandments. Keeping the commandments certainly entails a certain type of behavior. To suggest that hell is empty is at the very least, imprudent.

The other perspective of thinking about this notion is to believe that God's mercy and love for all of His creation is so great that in His own good time He will save all He has created, and bring all back to perfection, as it was in the beginning. We know from Genesis that God created everything good. For many who have seen beloved family members and friends fall away from the faith, or who have never embraced it, this is a very comforting idea. In order for it to work, we have to adopt assumptions for which we have no basis. We would have to suppose that God would give all who die in the state of mortal sin, or in a state of complete disbelief, a chance to repent either directly before or after death. He would give them sufficient grace to surmount their own wills, adopt His, profess sorrow, ask forgiveness, and be willing to accept His just punishment. Further, if all creation were to reach perfection, it would mean God would extend the offer to

Satan and the fallen angles, and all of them would repent and be saved. These are two very different and opposing perspectives, one to the extreme left and the other to the extreme right, which brings them together in the same position of no foundational support for their perspective views. The scriptures tell us God's ways are not our ways. We do not know exactly what God's ultimate plans are. It may well be in the realm of possibilities that God will not allow Satan to capture and lead to damnation any of His creation, including himself. We only know there will be a just judgment. The aforementioned subject is one about which we should not idly speculate; we should leave it in the hands of Almighty God.

Archbishop Vigano's case, which has caused further division in the Church, could easily have been avoided. The Pope and the Vatican were advised by many learned Catholics not to excommunicate the Archbishop. Instead, the Vatican chose to try him and declare that he has excommunicated himself by virtue of his actions. This is a thorny issue, and I am not aware of all the information, but from what I do know, I believe Archbishop Vigano will eventually be reinstated and exonerated. It is sad indeed to see clergy and laity lining up on one side or the other in opposition and causing further division in the Church. It is a situation that could not make the enemies of the Catholic Church happier. What follows is a further look at division.

Chapter Six

Division

Prior to my describing where this all leads, an identification of the fundamental and profound problem we face is in order; it can be characterized by one word: division. The division began in Heaven when Satan said he would not serve, revolted, and was expelled by St. Michael, the Archangel. That original division has continued with men here on earth. In his book *The Lord of the Rings*, Tolkien places these words in the mouth of Gandalf: 'Work of the Enemy!' said Gandalf. 'Such deeds he loves: friend at war with friend; loyalty divided in confusion of hearts.' A bit later, he adds the following: 'Ill deeds have been done here; but let all enmity that lies between you be put away, for it was contrived by the Enemy and works his will.' Here Tolkien gives us an insight into the spiritual enemy we face. Moreover, these passages exhort us to deny Satan his victory by refusing to divide ourselves. It seems a lesson we are incapable of learning.

Scripture tells us we are all created in the image and likeness of God; therefore, all men are brothers and friends. Our enemy, Lucifer, is certainly delighted to see friend at war with friend as exemplified in human history. Divisions abound, Theist vs Atheist, Christian vs non-Christian, Christian vs Christian, and Catholic vs Catholic; the splintering continues unabated. Gandalf's advice is full of wisdom, but not followed. In broad historical terms, the Protestant Revolt, the French revolution, the Russian Revolution, World War I and II, the rise of communism, the spread of secularism, and the sexual revolution all exemplify the division we suffer. All these conflicts have seen Christians attacked and/or killed by their fellow man. The division at best is scandal and shame; at worst, it is a crime. The source of the division is pride, and the source of pride is Satan. Some will argue Satan is a metaphor or symbol, but certainly not an actual entity that exists and exerts influence. Even some in the clergy take this position. However, if you believe what Jesus, the Christ, said (Luke 10:18), you quickly conclude that metaphors do not fall from heaven like lightning.

Chapter Six: Division

The division referred to arises from three major fault lines and all are related. The first and broadest among them is the division between those who believe in God and those who do not. The next is the division between Christianity and every other religion. The third can be split into two categories, and it is by far the most influential and most dangerous. The first category is the divide in Christianity, and the other, very closely related, is the divide in Catholicism. The reason the divides in Christianity and Catholicism are so dangerous is the fact that independently and collectively they exert enormous influence on everything else, which operates in a society; they inform every aspect of life in the culture. The fact that there is division drastically produces negative influences by allowing false narratives to step in and rule the day and night. The divisions act as though they were withdrawals or retreats.

Theoretically, resolving these divides seems to be a manageable process, which, with dedicated work, should yield success. Nevertheless, this is a notion realized only in the mind, or on the theoretical drawing board. Once one has to contend with these divisions on a practical level, overwhelming difficulties and barriers abound. What appears perfect in theory has and continues to fail completely in practice. It is prudent to remember that all Christians were initially Catholic. The failure of Christianity to remain united has led to catastrophe. Cited earlier are some examples of the current chaos. The current decline in the quality of all aspects of contemporary life is also a direct result of this division. The division itself diminishes the influence Christianity and specifically Catholicism can exert on a society. It is quite evident that contemporary society is being propelled forward by the notion that each individual creates his or her own reality, and that no outside objective reality exists. That is creating a virtual world without a Gameboy.

Over time, this delusion will grow so powerful that it will not be recognized as a delusion. We have the power to overcome this situation with the assistance of grace. When grace is given, we must use it. When God created both angels and men, He did not create them as automatons. If we had been created to be good by a design that achieved that end by allowing us no other choice, we would not be participants and would have no merit. We would choose the good only because we had no other choice. Only a personal, loving God would allow His creatures the dignity of participation and free choice. We were given a great gift, but it comes with great responsibility. We will consider the implications of free choice later in this volume. Let us consider a few facts as the movement toward the conclusion begins.

Before we explore the three identified fault lines of division, we must acknowledge an impediment. In Luke 12:51-53, Jesus tells us He has come not to bring peace, but separation. Our efforts at unity, even among Catholics, may well fall short of success, or may be impossible. Nevertheless, we should continue our efforts toward unity. Unity must be achieved by adhering to the principle of non-contradiction. Acceptance of a false ecumenism based on the error that all religions are paths to God will not lead to unity. The only acceptable unity must be with Christ and the Catholic Church. Our Lord knew not all would receive and embrace His message. Our duty is to spread His message, by love, to our neighbor and to all men: the rest we leave in His hands.

The first and most basic divide is between theists and atheists. Of course, one should never force someone to believe. The faith must be freely accepted. Neither those forced nor those doing the forcing benefit in any way. It is an approach that causes more harm than good for all parties involved. The Catholic Church has always, as part of its mission, worked for the salvation of all humanity. Spreading the Gospel throughout the world was the command Jesus gave his apostles, and to us, through apostolic succession. The Catholic Church must continue to proclaim loudly the Gospel in the public square with confidence and vigor. At the same time, we must acknowledge that some will not believe. The Church must continue to pray for them, which is to say all Catholics should be praying for those who do not believe. Our Lord came to save the lost sheep. We must continue to join Him in that mission.

The second fault line is the division among religions. We have monotheists and polytheists, Catholics, Protestants, Jews, Islamists, and a wide variety of other faiths. Again, here we face the same dilemma we read about in Luke 12:51-53. Some will not accept Jesus as the Christ, the Son of God. We need to cooperate with our fellow man, and to be sure, there will always be areas and issues allowing us to cooperate even with those who most oppose us, and work against us on most issues. Our duty is to evangelize with love and spread the Gospel of Christ. Whether it is accepted or not is beyond our control. The evangelized then bear the burden of responsibility.

The third fault line is the division that exists between Christians: Catholics and Protestants. There are numerous divisions among Protestants, and the same splintering is happening among Catholics. It is a situation in need of repair. At the time of writing (2024), what divides us is substantial. We are not arguing about whether we should kneel, stand or sit during the liturgy. We are arguing about issues, which either comport with or reject the teaching of Jesus. If not addressed properly and with alacrity, we will experience more division. Martin Luther once said if you sin, sin mightily. He based this statement on his notion that Jesus by his death on the cross has saved all Christians, and behavior even though sinful will not change that fact. By this one statement, he proves himself to be a fabulist. It is a clear logical and theological error; nevertheless, it had an abducent influence on Pope Francis.

Non-believers

The most obvious form of a non-Catholic is a non-believer, and it is appropriate to address this category first. There are a variety of unbeliefs: agnostics, atheists, and militant atheists. It is our Christian duty to pray for them. We pray that their freedom of choice will be open to the grace freely provided by God. Prayer must also take place in the form of action; we must proclaim the Gospel to them when we interact. We understand we must rule out force, as a means of promoting our faith and that conversion must be accomplished with concern for all our fellow travelers. Charity must be the basis of all our evangelizing efforts to spread the faith. We are in a battle, but violence of any type is not in our arsenal; we have a more potent weapon, the truth, Christ, Our Lord. He is the way, the truth, and the life.

In practical terms, whether an agnostic, who is uncertain if there is a God, an atheist, who is certain there is no God, or a militant atheist, who actively works to destroy all religious belief, the posture held by all of them has devastatingly negative effects on society. When one denies God, one also denies there are any fixed parameters by which to conduct a life. This leads to engaging in behaviors that violate the commandments of God and cause wreckage in the fabric of life. Thievery, infidelity, pornography, injustice, and physical and economic violence, etc., are woven into the fabric of life when God is disregarded. Disregarded is any idea of moral absolutes. The progressive decline occurs, in many cases, very slowly, and in minute increments over time. By this process, the degradation is unnoticed by most, even though all suffer daily from the results.

As a matter of practicality, in our daily lives, we must all profess our faith by resisting and pushing back against any, and all elements in the society and culture which deny God's presence. We have identified the enemy. How, as Catholics, do we combat this enemy of Christ? First, by remembering what St. Paul tells us in Ephesians 6:12: 'For our wrestling is not against flesh and blood; but against principalities and powers, against the rulers of the world of this darkness, against the spirits of wickedness in the high places.' Paul is informing us that these powers influence the thoughts and actions of men. Therefore, we know we must attempt to correct, and that we must achieve the correction, with charity, in other words, with love. Our criticism must not be to destroy, but to lead our fellow man to God. Each of us must engage, teach, and pray, in the variety of ways in which each is capable, to help those most in need.

When I consider what differentiates those who believe in God from those who do not, two thoughts come to mind. One is Pandora's Box, and the other is Guardian Angels. I will start with Guardian Angels. As a young boy in Catholic grammar school, I found the Nuns were fond of teaching us that we each had the protection of a Guardian Angel. Moreover, this Angel, sent to us by God, was constantly directing us toward good thoughts and actions. At the same time, there was an evil angel bombarding us with directions to move us away from God. The image they described for us was an angel of light sitting on one shoulder, and an angel of darkness sitting on the opposite shoulder. They explained to us that one reason the nuns, priests, and our parents were here was to instruct us on how to constantly listen to and follow the directions from the good angel while ignoring the bad one. It was our introduction to the spiritual world surrounding us. It was a notion that was no longer preached by the time I reached 8th grade. The result of which led to a poverty in understanding the spiritual dimension of reality; it is a poverty, which remains to this day.

Why the Church became shy about teaching such a fundamental reality is a confusing issue. It certainly has to do with secularism leaching into the Church in the form of modernism, Liberation theology, and unrestrained individualism. Perhaps the emphasis on individualism is the most dangerous because it leads to the substitute of arbitrary personal doctrines for the doctrines of Christ. How did so many in the hierarchy of the Church fall prey to a distorted theology? I will address this question later on. The picture of the angels, which the Nuns presented to us, has helped us as adults to understand that even though we believe in God, we are in a battle every day. It is a battle that we can win only through prayer. Catholics who grew up in the Church after Vatican II most likely never think of or even know they have guardian angels and may not realize they are in a spiritual battle every day.

Now back to considering Pandora's Box. Before opening Pandora's Box and releasing evil, those who deny God first empty themselves. Once one has eliminated God, there remains only a vacancy, a hollow man. That vacancy is filled with the evils released from Pandora's Box; the key, which opens the box, is denying God. The Catholic Church, for centuries, has been a bulwark standing in opposition to the evils coming out of that box. Since Vatican II, the Church has let down its guard. This has allowed those evils to seep into every aspect of our society, and into the Church itself. The chilling effect has been the constant elimination of the Christian ethic operating in the worldwide culture. We will be unable to overcome this juggernaut unless the members in the Church hierarchy regain their courage and once again proclaim the Doctrines of Christ in the public square.

Christianity and other Religions

It is only with Christianity, and we will leave Judaism aside for now, that we have a religion established by God. Buddha, Mohamed, Luther, Cranmer, Calvin, and every other originator of a religion, religious movement, philosophical practice, or any other practice or method used for conducting one's life is a mere human being. Christianity is the only religion established by God, who then came into the physical world He created to save His creation. Christ said: "I am the way, and the truth, and the life. No man cometh to the Father, but by me" (John 14:6). Throughout history, God has shed His grace on all of humanity, and bits of truth have been expressed in all quarters. With the coming of the Messiah, the fullness of truth became physically present. Before He ascended into Heaven, Jesus met the eleven disciples:

> "And Jesus coming, spoke to them, saying: All power is given to me in heaven and on earth. Going therefore, teach ye all nations, baptizing them in the name of the Father,

> and of the Son, and of the Holy Ghost. Teaching them to observe all things whatsoever I have commanded you: and Behold I am with you all days, even to the consummation of the world." (Matthew 28:18-20)

Christianity is not some cleverly devised creation of one or more brilliant human minds; its source is God, and its power comes from God. Evangelization of all of humanity is a command from Christ, because God's love extends to all human beings, and he desires to save all His creation. Spreading the Gospel is an act of love in which Christians participate when they evangelize. We worship God formally when we attend the Mass in Church, but in addition, we must follow His command and worship God by spreading the Gospel to all men. We cannot force anyone to believe, but we must present the message to fulfill our duty as Christians. Knowing that we follow the light, we cannot help but attempt to bring those in darkness into the light. This is the dialogue that needs to occur, a dialogue of drawing in all men to Christ, Jesus. As Catholics, we should practice and profess the faith with clarity, confidence, and enthusiasm in private conversations and in the public square. Christianity is not a particular file among many files to be stored away from the conduct of life. It is the life giving force we need to use throughout the world in order to transform it. It is the path to life.

Christianity and Judaism

With Judaism, we come to a special case. Unlike every other religion, it is from Judaism that Christianity springs. Therefore, Judaism is a religion whose source is God. Only Judaism and Christianity share this source. Jesus, the Messiah, the Son of God is born a Jew. He came to fulfill the law and the prophets, and to save mankind. As St. John tells us, He came to His own and His own received Him not. The fact that the Jews rejected Jesus and continue to do so is a tragedy. Of course, not all Jews rejected Jesus. After the resurrection and descent of the Holy Ghost, the apostles, many other Jews, and pagans became followers of Jesus. They are Christians and initially all Christians were Catholics. After the destruction of the Temple in 70 AD, the end of the priesthood, the loss of the Ark of the Covenant, which occurred earlier, and the dispersal of the Jews throughout the nations of the earth, Judaism transformed over time into a religion based on the Talmud. The ancient Israelites had believed in a religion based on the Torah. Modern Talmudic Judaism has very little in common with the ancient Israelites. Religious Jews are a minority among the majority who have become secularized and either indifferent or completely non-believing. The Zionist movement is a political movement not a religious one. Since most Jews reject the fact that Jesus was the Messiah and the Son Of God, many are still waiting for the arrival of an earthly messiah. Since they rejected Jesus, Jews have been a force, among others, to undermine Christianity, and Christian society. This has proven disastrous for both Christians and Jews. Of all people on earth, Jews should be the most enthusiastic of Christians. Christ came into the world first for them. Tragically, they remain separated. Many Jews have converted to Christianity in general or to Catholicism in particular over the centuries, and conversions continue to occur. Those who remain Jews rather than following God's plan will be shocked at the second coming of the Messiah. They will see and realize for the first time that Jesus who was given to them by the Father, whom they had crucified, is their promised Messiah. As Christians we pray for the conversion of the Jews, and the scriptures indicate before the end they will be converted. We have these words of Jesus: "Because I came down from heaven, not to do my will, but the will of him that sent me. Now this is the will of the Father who sent me: that of all that he hath given me, I should lose nothing; but should raise it up again in the last day" (John 6:38-39). We pray that the Father give all Jews, all Christians, and all men to the Son, so that Our Lord will lose none of us.

Christianity and Catholicism

As tragic as all this separation and disunity is, the most tragic is the division among Christians. When Luther initiated the Protestant Revolt (I refer to it as a revolt because Luther broke with the Catholic Church and with the teaching of Jesus), it was the first division among the multitude of divisions that have occurred in Protestantism since. Because there is no official head and no magisterium, continual splintering is the result. With each split, the prospect of reconciliation with the Catholic Church becomes more remote and difficult. There is no real effort to meet and work on a process to overcome objections and move toward a genuine reconciliation. There are ecumenical services, which unfortunately are shallow shows with no depth. Both sides are comfortable with playing at cooperation which, when it comes to reconciliation, is feeble or dead.

While the Protestants continue to splinter into more and more denominations, the current Catholic hierarchy charts a course down the same road by means of synodality. If this continues, there will be final unity among Catholics and Protestants; they will be hollow Christians, having arrived at a state of non-belief. This is an assured distorted unity if both stay on the present course. This is both a tragedy and a crime. The Catholic hierarchy as well as the Protestant clergy will have much explaining to God about why they did not correct this division. They are called to simply follow the doctrines of Christ rather than to create their own doctrines. It appears they all love authority as long as they wield it but are reluctant to yield to the authority of the King of Kings.

Catholics

When I was growing up in the late 1940's and early 1950's, I recall one Holy Catholic and Apostolic Church, and I emphasize the word one. It now appears the Church has taken on the characteristics of an umbrella. There are three factional churches under its cover. There is the church of nice, the synodal church, and the traditional church. By far, the largest group of Catholics belongs to the church of nice. Most of them are observant and devout, and many are able to detect error when they hear or see it. In many places, they are misled by the hierarchy but go along with it because it comes from a priest or bishop, whose authority they respect. In addition, they are advised to refrain from responding. They are slowly being led away from the foundations of the Catholic Faith, but it is not noticeable. Most of the members of the church of nice are oblivious to the alterations being attempted by the synodal church, and decidedly uninterested in the traditional church. The synodal church has the fewest members; however, it has the most power and influence. The synodal church is attempting to create some type of new church, with no sure idea of where it will continue to go. We need a correction; it will come according to God's will. The traditional church is attempting to preserve the faith as received, accepting change, but not destroying tradition in the process. Catholics find they are no longer one, and confusion and separation are common place. The traditional church is growing. The Latin Mass is attended by old and young alike; it is one of the few places to see teenagers at Mass, and traditional seminaries are filled with prospects. These three factions will eventually unite because in the heart of every Catholic is a thirst for Our Lord Jesus. That unity will come, but we know not when.

I am reluctant and sorry to say that the Vatican under Pope Francis instead of promoting unity in the Catholic Church promoted division. Pope Francis was not the origin of division, but during his pontificate he abetted, enabled, and encouraged the trend. Wittingly or unwittingly, he found or created problems that did not exist. One example is the effort to eliminate the Traditional Latin Mass. Anyone who has been following current events in the Church is aware of several other examples. Tragically, he cleverly maneuvered a transfer of the fault of division to traditionally-minded Catholics. On several occasions, he accused them of rigidity and division. This is another example of creating a problem that did not exist. As mentioned above, the Catholic Church has always been a force countering evil and promoting a moral culture. At present, there is confusion about what some officials in the Church consider moral. In fact, after the election of Pope Francis, the hierarchy sowed theological confusion. In this confused state, many Catholics have embraced support of abortion, transgenderism, gay marriage, and women priests. If Catholics are confused and conflicted, is there any chance that those who do not believe in God will be persuaded by those they can plainly see do not believe themselves!

As Catholics, we face several challenges. The challenges faced by the Church are formidable. If the Church is to grow, all Catholics must work to surmount them. Like our Protestant brothers, we are causing divisions among ourselves. One of the major divisions is in doctrine; the other major division is in the practice of the faith. Each influences the other. If the doctrines become distorted or devalued, the practice of the faith will follow in like manner. If the practices are altered in ways that diminish sacredness, the theology will slowly be altered, adapting itself to the practice. The doctrines we must follow are the doctrines of Christ and the traditions of the Church. That is what we refer to as the deposit of faith.

We recite the basic doctrines of faith when we recite the creed at Mass. In addition to those doctrines, we adhere to others based on scripture and tradition. To list a few, we believe marriage is between one man and one woman, that we must not steal, commit adultery, or bear false witness, that our actions should be just, that abortion is murder and a mortal sin, and that we must be in the state of grace to receive the Eucharist. Disagreements about these types of theological issues lead to division. We practice our faith through prayer, Mass, and the sacraments. Disagreements about these also lead to division.

Chapter Six: Division

There are those in the Church (and it is not just a recent phenomenon) who believe it is their job to edit and revise the Word of God. They are mistaken; it is not the job at all. Their job, as well as ours, is to practice, preserve, and pass on God's Word. I have mentioned synodality earlier in this volume. Synodality is another word for relativism. Those in charge favor the term because it sounds neutral and avoids the negative associations connected to relativism. It allows for making changes gradually, which go unnoticed by most, and reduces the amount of resistance to a small minority. The synodal process deserves nothing less than elimination as a method of running the Church. Synodality is nothing other than Catholicism's version of what the Talmud is for Judaism, and what Sola Scriptura, scripture alone, is for Protestants. The Talmudic approach led to a great loss of faith among Jews; by faith alone has achieved the same wreckage among Protestants; synodality will achieve the same result among Catholics, if it is not abandoned. Synodality will lead to (as Thomas Huxley so aptly characterized the religion of Aguste Comte) "Catholicism minus Christianity." In fact, in the Church today it is readily observable that Synodality is creating a cultural Catholicism, emphasizing man, rather than a religious Catholicism, emphasizing God. The influence has already misled many, and it will spread disease through the entire Church unless we end it. One of the primary reasons for the unity in the Catholic Church is the fact that we have the office of the papacy. Under the guidance of the Holy Ghost, the Pope has the final word when it comes to theological matters. The Pope does not have arbitrary authority; it is not a personal authority or the authority of the office itself. The Pope is subject to the Authority of Christ, and he must use that authority adhering to the doctrines of Christ. Without this central authority, which must be wielded subject to Christ, a pope or individual bishops would be able to arbitrarily practice and create their own religions. They would determine which doctrines of Christ they would follow and which they would dismiss. The logical extension of the synodal path leads to a dead end, bringing all who follow it to a posture of nonbelief. Do not follow that path.

Who am I that I should disagree with and ignore the directives of this or any other Pope? Answer, I am nobody. It is quite an unpleasant thought to conclude the pontiff is wrong. Considering I am nobody, or even if I were somebody, why would I do such an unsavory thing? Because I was brought up in the Catholic faith. I was taught that my allegiance is first and foremost to God. I believe that with every fiber of my being, and I know when I hear deviations from the Catholic faith. When those deviations are issued by a high authority, even if it happens to be the Holy Father, they cannot be ignored. I am a small, insignificant voice; however, there are many important voices who see danger in this pontificate and in the Church.

Within the Catholic Church we have several unfortunate, sorrowful, and serious divides; one is the divide and separation between mainstream Catholics and Sedevacantist Catholics. I have a great deal of sympathy for these Catholics who hold on to tradition but are outside the Church, that is, not in communion with Rome. My brother and I were discussing this tragedy, and he brought up a cogent and salient point; it is exactly why I admire the Sedevacantists but cannot join them. My brother noted that Sedevacantists argue that Jesus separated himself from the mainstream of Judaism in His day. To say Jesus separated Himself or revolted in the same sense that Martin Luther revolted from the Catholic Church is a misnomer. Jesus came to the Jewish authorities and people to get them back on track. They had strayed from the path God had planned for them since the time of Abraham. Christ did not separate Himself from Judaism, nor did He come to reform it: He corrected it according to the will of the Father. After the Israelites entered the Promised Land, God sent prophets to keep them on the correct path, but those prophets were ignored or abused. The Father then sent the Word into the world.

Jesus must have said to the Pharisees, Sadducees, Scribes, and Priests on many occasions that they had substituted the doctrines of God for the doctrines of men. It was the hierarchy in the religion and the most highly educated among the Jews who rejected Jesus as the Messiah. With no possibility of reform from within, Christianity was born. It was not the replacement of Judaism; it was the continuation of the path God intended for all men from the call of Abraham. It was a call to the Jews to fol-

Chapter Six: Division

low the doctrines of God, and they refused to follow. Had the Jewish leaders accepted Jesus as the Christ, the Son of God, the history of the Church would most likely have been very different. The truth of Christ's message caused a break with Judaism through the creation of Christianity, which is the fulfillment and continuation of God's call to Abraham. That fulfillment is in the Holy Roman Catholic Church.

The Sedevacantists find themselves in a position similar to the one Jesus faced. With no possibility of reform from within the Church, especially while under the papacy of Francis, they decided to hold onto the Church's traditional teaching outside the official Church. Their criticisms of current trends in the Church are certainly valid and deserving of careful consideration by the hierarchy. The Catholic Church should make efforts to reconcile the differences and mend this split. The hurdles unification would face should not dissuade the effort to pursue the goal.

As my brother and I discussed this issue, we concluded that while the criticisms and arguments of the Sedevacantists are well-founded, their decision to leave the Church is not. They might point to Jesus and say that He broke away from Judaism for legitimate reasons and that they are doing the same. They have not thought this out well enough. As noted above, Jesus did not break away from the established Jewish religion; He was God incarnate, full of mercy and wisdom. He set it back on the correct path, the path He had planned from the beginning. We should never break away from the Church; we are not gods. All Catholics including Sedevacantists should be working inside the Church to restore the balance, no matter how frustrating it happens to be. We may fail to make the necessary corrections in our lifetime, but the essential factor is that we be loyal to the doctrines of Christ and carry on and defend the deposit of the faith as it was handed on to us. We cannot allow the world to influence the Church; the Church must influence the world.

The Eucharist is of such importance in the life of the Church that it is worthwhile to restate what can and should be done to promote belief in the real presence and bring about true Eucharistic revival. The fact that belief in the real presence of God in the Eucharist must be resuscitated among Catholics, even those who attend Church weekly, or more frequently, is a great shame, if not a crime. I say there is serious talk about a revival, and from the hierarchy, that is all it is: talk, because thus far the path to the revival they are pursuing will yield no results in restoring belief in the real presence. Those among the clergy, and there are many, who would institute the steps outlined below are silenced and thwarted in their efforts. Success towards this goal would be ensured if the following steps were to be implemented universally in the Church.

1) Move forward with the tabernacle in all churches at the center of the altar.
2) Eliminate all tables from the sanctuary.
3) Move forward to all traditional altars.
4) Say all masses Ad Orientem.
5) Install altar rails around the sanctuary.
6) Move forward only with the Traditional Latin Mass.
7) Eliminate communion in the hand.
8) Allow altar boys only.
9) Allow the priest or deacon only to distribute communion.

10) Allow readings & homilies to be done only by the clergy.
11) Require silence in church in the presence of God.
12) Require a Sunday best dress code for men, women, and children.
13) Use Gregorian chant and other sacred music only.
14) Establish choir lofts.

Instituting these would be a good start, for they would help to rebuild the sacredness of the church and sanctuary and the respect owed to God when we are in His presence in church. Many other adjustments should be made as time goes on, among them: restoration of the bell towers, the return of ambos in churches, women wearing veils, and in the U.S, the laity with missals in Latin and English for the Mass. Above, I have used the term "move forward" deliberately. Otherwise, I would be accused of wanting to move backwards; I want to move forward, but correctly. Moreover, as someone very wise once said, when you are about to drive over a cliff, the best path is backwards. In my humble opinion, the current leadership in the Church is recklessly speeding towards a chasm; the suggestions above will hopefully slow the pace and reverse the direction. Moreover, I believe they would eventually foster unity among all Catholics. No doubt, it would take time, but it would be the result.

The unity we seek is unity in the doctrines of Christ. All are welcome means we invite all of humanity into the Church to be transformed into the type of individuals about whom God can say what He had to say about David: "A man after my own heart." Simply put, we do not seek unity, which accepts a variety of opposing and contradictory positions, for the sake of getting along. We seek unity in the truth: Jesus and the Church that He established on earth. Any other type of supposed unity is false and doomed to failure.

Three Considerations

Free choice, altered theology, and damnation, which were mentioned previously, will be addressed now.

Free Choice

If you were to listen to a determinist, he would of course proclaim you have no free will and you never make a free choice. What you do and how you behave is controlled by infinitesimally small particles randomly interacting in the quantum world. This same determinist will tell women they have the right to choose life or death for a child in the womb. This is a dishonest approach on display for all to see. It violates the principle of non-contradiction. One either has the right to choose, therefore free choice exists, or if there is no free choice, then one has no right to choose. But it cannot be said that both exist at the same time. If you listen to God, who created all those particles in the quantum world, you will have made a much better choice. You will know that you have free will and you make free choices throughout your entire lifetime. In addition, you will never experience any contradictory statements from God. He has placed before us good and evil and tells us to choose the good. Ask that determinist how he came to believe there is no such thing as free choice, and he will tell you he chose to believe it!

Altered Theology

Watering down, perhaps dumbing down, is a more accurate way of describing what has been going on for a long time. Dumbing down is a more accurate assessment because when you substitute private subjective pronouncements for the pronouncements of God, that is dumb. Currently, we are experiencing a rash of faulty substitutions for the doctrines of God. Arbitrarily changing God's law or the deposit of the Catholic faith is a dangerous course for those making the changes and for those affected by them. It is a road better not taken. As many saints have proclaimed, remain faithful to Christ and His Church. The current hierarchy in the Catholic Church is enamored with constant change; they are suffering with a case of agathism. They are attempting to build a church that is divorced from The Holy Roman Catholic Church. The Synodal Church they are building and the moral tenets they are changing, or attempting to change, will fail unless God wills the success of what they are attempting. But dumbing down never leads to better results. When we pray at Mass for peace and unity in the Church, the prayer specifies according to the will of God. The current turmoil in the Church may be God's will for us at present. It may be a wakeup call out of slumber.

Damnation

To be sure, damnation is no happy prospect. The aegis of proper behavior should not be the fear of punishment, but one should be aware that the possibility exists. Rather than being concerned about being personally damned, our greatest fear or concern may be about the possible damnation of a loved one. Even knowing that God is perfectly just and merciful, the thought that a spouse, father, mother, brother, sister, another family member or cherished friend will be damned is a sorrowful prospect to contemplate. A final thought about the damnation of Satan. It is correct to say the Church teaches there is no salvation for Satan and the angels who followed him. We know Satan was created good, but he chose to rebel. Perhaps, rather than an eternity in hell, separated from God, the most severe and humiliating punishment for Satan might be his kneeling before God expressing sorrow, asking for forgiveness, and accepting God's just punishment. God might forgive him, and all would return to good as it was in the beginning. We do not know the mind of God, but one day we will know His plan for creation and how it was worked out.

Consent

I have not referred to the argument for consent earlier in this volume. This is number four of three considerations; as my friend said, you must have been a math major. It needs to be addressed because it is a false argument. The fact that an individual, a couple, or a group of people consent to some sort of sexual perversion or some other evil action, and by virtue of consent, the legitimacy of the action is granted, is a complete and utter fallacy. Yet, it is a widely accepted working principle in the general society, and it has crept silently into the thinking of many in the Church. Consent of an individual or a group, in an illegal or immoral action, rather than granting approval, screams loudly of guilt. It is a tacit acknowledgement that one is guilty and has sinned against God and man. It implies that one understands that one has broken the law of God and besmirched the dignity of man. The embrace of this notion confirms the fact that once God has been dismissed, all propositions and behaviors become acceptable. It is one more nail in the coffin of a society which is slowly dying because of its excesses.

Immigration

Since I have already demonstrated that I do not understand that three considerations do not mean four, I might as well compound the error by adding comments about immigration as the fifth of three. Illegals crossing the borders have caused a great deal of difficulty for many Americans for a long time. An analogy will be illustrative.

A school can accept 800 students in the next academic year. One thousand apply, and for this experiment we will say each of them has a perfect score on the entrance exam. Unfortunately, two hundred will have to be denied entrance because there is no room for more than eight hundred. To make it as fair as possible, each student is assigned a number in a blind random process, and then those numbers are chosen in the same manner. The first 800 students chosen will be accepted. Two hundred others will have to attend another school, but if they choose to transfer in the following year they will be the first to be accepted. If these common sense principles were applied to a nation's immigration policy it would create a system which would be just for all. Justice is what should prevail, but do not hold your breath. We are in short supply of justice because large segments of our society have abandoned the reality of objective moral standards based on the law of God.

Seismic Events

It appears to me, history has moved forward due to lynchpin events that have resulted in paradigm shifts. Thus far, I see three such events and all a result of a great flaw. The first, was the rejection of God by Lucifer; the second, with the help of Lucifer, the rejection of God by Adam and Eve; the third the rejection of God by the Jews, His chosen people, and all have had disastrous results throughout human history. The possibility exists that there may be one more such lynchpin event, which will equal in its scope the disastrous effects of the first three. There are signs that the next rejection of God will occur again among His people, this time by those who bear His name, Christians. The Words of Our Lord: "I say to you, that he will quickly revenge them. But yet the Son of man, when he cometh, shall he find, think you, faith on earth?" (Luke 18: 8). In the past, I surmised this passage to be a rhetorical question posed by Jesus. Based on the conditions in the world and inside the Church, I now see it more as a description of what the King of Kings will find on earth when He returns. I hope that impression is wrong; it would indeed be very sad to see such a great loss of faith. This volume is a clarion call to avoid this being the case. It is difficult not to notice the storm clouds that are gathering, and it is possible we, as were Sts. Peter and Paul in their day, will be overwhelmed by the conditions around us. Though we may suffer martyrdom and appear to be defeated, we know that the outcome is God's complete victory. In that is our hope and salvation.

Of course, there are two more seismic events, which dwarf these three occurrences and every other event in history: The birth and resurrection of Jesus, the Son of God, who is God. In the history of the planet, there are no events as important, or even come close to the magnitude of the implications of these two events. It has brought the possibility of life to all, even to those who do not realize it. They are miracles, unapproachable and unsurpassable, and should elicit a prayer of thanks as often as we inhale. That can easily be done by considering all our thoughts and actions as prayers of thanksgiving.

Chapter Seven

Be a Catholic / Become a Catholic

There is only one reason why I have addressed the problems and controversies we are currently experiencing in the Catholic Church. It is because the rest of this volume will be a rigorous affirmation of the fact that the only way to the Father and Heaven is through Jesus, the Christ. It is the path of the Catholic Church. In the search for truth, we must be perfectly honest; therefore, the list of our problems. Those I hope to convince must know we are no better than are any of our fellows. In the Church, we have problems and controversies, but the mistakes and errors of individuals, no matter their positions, do not in any way diminish or damage the efficacy of Christ or His Church. Those convinced by the argument to join should know they join a Church that struggles and groans to satisfy and spread the Word of God. They will enter a Church filled with men and women dedicated to Christ—a Church filled with people, whose aim is to attain sainthood.

The balance of this volume will concentrate on why everyone should be a Catholic, and why the Catholic Church is the one and only true Church. If one is a Catholic, it means being fully Catholic. One must fully profess the doctrines of Christ, accept the deposit of the faith, and adhere to the Magisterium of the Church. If not a Catholic, one should seek to become a member of the Church established by the Son of God. It is legitimate to ask, in the face of the problems listed, how can I make this recommendation? The recommendation is made because the Church remains inviolable; it is under the protection of the Holy Ghost. We have Christ's promise that He would never abandon His Church. The Church consists of all the members who faithfully adhere to all the doctrines of Christ. "If you love me, keep my commandments. And I will ask the Father, and he shall give you another Paraclete, that he may abide with you forever" (John 14: 15-16). Some of this adherence to Jesus, the Son of God, who is God is visible, and much of it is invisible. Throughout the history of the Church, human persons, some of whom have been faithful, some of whom have not been, have headed the institution. Human persons

Chapter Seven: Be a Catholic / Become a Catholic

can and do fall into error; when they happen to have leadership roles in the Church, the defect lies in the human persons, not in the Church. False teaching resides in the person, not in the body of the Church. The Church has had wolves in sheep's clothing within it since the beginning, and we currently have them. However, they cannot and will not prevail. It is important that we pray for the conversion of all the lost sheep and shepherds.

The angel Gabriel's announcement to Mary that she will conceive of the Holy Spirit, the birth of Jesus, the flight into Egypt, the miracles Christ performed, the transfiguration, the death of Jesus on the cross, His resurrection and ascension, are all chronicled in the New Testament. Nevertheless, all these events occurred in the Old Testament or in Old Testament times. This is critically important for several reasons, three of which are momentous; after the miracle of creation, the most important miracles in the Old Testament are the immaculate conception of Mary, her incarnation, and the resurrection of Christ. In addition, we have insights into the apostles' understanding of Jesus as the Messiah. As mentioned above, it is only after the resurrection and the descent of the Holy Ghost on Pentecost, that the apostles understand that Jesus was God. The entire weight of the Old Testament proclaimed that God was a Spirit Being; no believing Jew could conceive of the notion of God as also human. Therefore, the Pharisees, Sadducees, and the priests found it impossible to believe Jesus, accept Him and believe he was God incarnate. Jesus came first to save the Jews and then all other men. Most of the Jews rejected Jesus, and now we are witnessing, in the 21st century, Christianity rejecting Jesus in the strongest possible terms: not practicing the faith in the world outside of Church. St. James tells us faith without works is dead. There is faith inside the churches, but it is practiced insufficiently in the practical world outside the churches. One example of this: When have you heard any member of the clergy decry the practice of usury? To say usury is evil, in church, is following the faith. Where are the works in public to eliminate this practice? Where is the practical effort to organize the laity to start insisting, in our legislation and institutions, that no lender, no matter who it is, should be allowed to charge more than 5% interest? In fact, the normal rate should be no more than 2 ½%. In addition, if lending money to friends and family, there should be no interest charged. This would be one example of bringing the Gospel of Truth into the public square. This is the type of real effort that needs to occur if we are to save the faith. In fact, if we thought of all men as our brothers there would be no interest charges for lending money.

A second example is also in order. When have you heard the clergy preaching against violence and war? Catholics should be hearing frequently from the pulpit that they should be working in the capacities they hold, to eliminate violence and war. We need to support congressmen and senators who support the idea that the United States should not be involved in proxy wars, or in funding or providing military equipment to foreign nations engaged in endless conflicts. Catholics in prominent and influential positions in the government, military, industry, and media should constantly be working to eliminate war and violence. It is the duty of the clergy to emphasize this point and the duty of the laity to accomplish it. This is not an easy or simple endeavor. There will be much resistance to this effort, and among the chief reasons is the fact that it will affect the billions of dollars generated by developing and providing weapons across the globe. We will be hated in many quarters for opposing war and violence, but, as the poem says, we should do it anyway. We will be accused of being isolationists, a loaded term designed to delegitimize the effort to avoid war. As Catholics, it could be said we are all isolationists; we are constantly about isolating ourselves from the wiles of Satan. We want to avoid sin and evil; therefore, we want to avoid war.

The Gospels were written after all the events in the life of Jesus occurred. The fulfillment of God's promise to Abraham, in the person of Jesus, is chronicled in the four Gospels. If one accepts that the story of Abraham is true, and the story of Moses is true, it follows that one then believes the Old Testament is true. The Old Testament being true proves the story of Jesus is true. Both Abraham and Moses lead to Jesus. No less astounding than the story of Abraham and Moses is the incident of the Transfiguration. In the Transfiguration, we see Moses and Elias representing the law and the prophets being fulfilled in Jesus. We have the Father, Son, and Holy Ghost; we have Abraham, Moses, and Jesus; we have Jesus, Elias, and Moses, and to this we add the three crucial historical events fully concentrated on Jesus: His birth, resurrection, and ascension. When Jesus ascends into heaven, He sends the Holy Ghost into the world to guide the Church. Three continuing conditions prevail due to the Ascension: we have the Holy Spirit of God with us, and we have Jesus advocating for us to the Father, and we have Jesus present in the Eucharist. All of this is in the scriptures. St. John also tells us at the end of his relaying of the Gospel that Jesus did many things not contained in the written Gospels (John 21:25). It is why Tradition is of extreme importance also. Scripture and Tradition have always guided the Catholic Church.

This all leads to the penultimate either/or. One of those is to dismiss Abraham, Moses, and Jesus as simply storytelling, mere fiction. The other is to realize the story of Abraham, Moses, and Jesus leads to two fundamental conclusions. First, the line of logic, the line of reason, the line of time, and the line of the Old Testament confirm Jesus as the Messiah, the Son of God, the King of Kings, and the transfiguration confirms that the law and the prophets are fulfilled in Jesus. Second, Jesus is now the living Passover from death to life. From Him and through apostolic succession, the Holy Roman Catholic Church becomes the vehicle through which we achieve salvation. Each of us must decide that Jesus is the Messiah or not. A non-decision is equal to joining the enemy. The enemy, of course, is the devil, and he uses humans as his surrogates. Since his rebellion, he has constantly opposed God and enlisted as many humans as will listen to him, to be damned. More was explored about damnation earlier in the section Three Considerations.

If one acknowledges Jesus as the Messiah, then one must embrace the one Holy Catholic and Apostolic Church. It means that one fully accepts both the Old Testament, which throughout points to Jesus, and the New Testament, which fulfills the Old. It requires one to live a life directed by a code of conduct based on God's law of love. This is the choice to make for Jews, all Christians, Muslims, atheists, and every other human being, no matter of what philosophical or religious persuasion. It leads

Chapter Seven: Be a Catholic / Become a Catholic

to an eternal life with God. In the meantime, it would create a wonderful situation on the earth.

To conclude that Jesus is not the Messiah, the Son of God, is a massive error. In fact, it is catastrophic. The implications indicate that one dismisses the New Testament. Having done that, one will also dismiss the Old Testament. Once there, there is nowhere to turn; one becomes a nihilist, determinist, and materialist. If there are no Old and New Testaments, there is no Jesus, the Messiah; there is no God; life has no meaning. Welcome to modernism; get as much of everything you want, as fast as you can, by any means you can, because you have accepted the idea that all behaviors are equal. When this situation occurs, societies and civilizations crumble under the crushing power of complete dystopia. It appears we are rapidly approaching this tipping point. Throughout history, the so-called elites have attempted to control their fellows; they have succeeded only on the parochial level, but the organizations and technologies that now exist may allow them to take complete control. This, of course, leads to the logical outcome or conclusion that results from denying the existence of God: we are the gods, we control everything; our science and technology will allow us to overcome every hurdle; eventually we will solve the disease of death, which will confirm that we in fact are the gods, because we will live forever. This is a choice only for the totally ignorant or insane. It is dismissing from ourselves all that is good and wholesome, and then opening Pandora's Box releasing all the evils, and giving them an invitation to enter.

God gives His grace freely to every human being; the part we play is to accept that grace. When it comes directly to the point of the choice, it is either/or. We are presented with a wager, or gamble, which is a way of referring to it in its crudest terms. It is Pascal's wager to which I refer. One can choose to believe there is a God and live according to His directions, or one can deny the existence of God. This choice can also apply about being a member of the Catholic Church. Shakespeare comes to mind: "To be or not to be."

If one chooses to gamble, denying the existence of God, and refuses to join the Catholic Church, one has chosen the side of the wager, which has no possibility of a win. At the very least, choosing the opposite side of the wager there is a 50/50 chance of winning. My position is that choosing God and the Catholic Church gives you a 100% chance of winning. God will not abandon you; the great danger is that you can choose to refuse His grace and abandon Him.

Denying the existence of God leaves one no other choice but to be a nihilist or determinist. Atheists themselves will tell you that physical forces, atoms interacting with each other, etc., control all of us. They deny free will, and of course believe that when we die we simply decompose and have reached our end. If there is nothing else, you had better get everything you want while you are alive. Entering on this side of the wager, one knows the only result is a loss. Therefore, there is no logical reason to choose this side of the wager. In a similar vein, our taking the position that all religions are equally valid and that the Catholic Church is not the only path to the Father and Heaven as revealed to us by Christ places one in a similar no win position.

If you insist on considering this a wager, then place your wager on God and the Catholic Church; at very least there is a 50/50 chance of winning. This of course is the bare minimum approach. For those of us who are Catholics we know faithfully following the doctrines of Christ, Jesus, and the teaching and traditions of the Catholic Church assure us of victory. If the atheist is correct, we lose nothing more than he does and neither of us has the satisfaction of knowing he was correct. On the other hand, if the atheist is wrong, he may be in for a tough time explaining to God why in spite of all the grace provided, he still refused to acknowledge God. This holds true for those choosing not to join the Catholic Church.

The other option, of course, is that we will know we were correct in our wager. The question then becomes, why bet on a position that has no possibility of a win, especially when the opposite position ensures a win? Your experience may be similar to mine. I have never encountered anyone who was willing to take a bet when they knew, in advance, that there was no possibility of winning. Even when there is the slimmest chance of winning, for example the lottery, many will take the chance hoping to be the lucky one this time. Even though slim, there is a chance. Betting against God ensures a loss, and the position of those who hold and act on a conviction that by its very nature confirms a loss in advance is irrational and illogical. Either emotional immaturity or evil are the source of such a choice.

Everything I have said is based on the following profound reasons why everyone should believe in God and be a member of the Catholic Church. All the problems I listed in the previous chapter collectively do not amount to even a mere trivial concern. The Catholic Church is founded on Christ, His vicar on earth is the Pope, and the Holy Ghost guides the Church.

First, all of nature on Earth and indeed the entire Universe confirms the existence of God. "The fool hath said in his heart: There is no God" (Psalm 13). You may be familiar with the story about the two physicists who were good friends. One believed in God, the other did not. The physicist who believed in God had just purchased a beautiful grandfather clock with a glass casing which allowed the entire mechanism to be seen. One afternoon the physicist who was an atheist visited his friend and commented what a magnificent piece of work it was. He then asked, 'Where did you get it?' His friend replied, 'Get it, I didn't get it anywhere; all of the components simply appeared, assembled themselves, and started working.' The atheist replied 'That is absurd, things like that do not happen.' His friend said, 'But my friend that is precisely what you believe about the universe.'

Second, all of science indicates there is a creator, whom we call God. Read Fr. Robert Spitzer's *Science at the Doorstep to God* for an insight into how science proves there is a God. Scientists who rely on only what they can observe without acknowledging there may be something beyond the limits of what is observable or imaginable will never realize that science demonstrates God exists. Imagine a group of scientists who live in flatland. If they never theorize that there may be other dimensions besides the one in which they are restricted, they will never conclude the science they can do demands dimensions beyond their empiricism.

Third, we have limits. The simplest example is sound. All of us hear within a certain range. There are pitches so high and so low we are incapable of hearing them. It would be a colossal error to conclude anything we do not hear does not exist. Sight and speed provide another example. If you have ever been stopped at a railroad crossing by a 100-car freight train, you see the engine and every car. However, if that 100-car train were moving close to the speed of light you would not see it. It would pass before your eyes as if it did not exist. These are examples of cautionary tales advising that we should be reluctant to conclude there is no God. Reason informs us that there is much which exists about which we know nothing. We should not automatically dismiss what we cannot observe or understand.

Fourth, in the entire history of man on the Earth no one has seen a resurrection from the dead, except for Jesus, the Christ. Other than the relatively small number of humans who actually saw Christ after He rose, the rest of humanity has a story about His resurrection but has never seen such an event happen. Here again we have thousands of years of empirical evidence confirming rising from the dead does not happen. Once again, we are confined to the limits of what we are capable of observing. We have proof of the resurrection and ascension of Our Lord, but if we confine ourselves to our limited empiricism, we will not believe the reality that it occurred. Those unable or unwilling to acknowledge a spiritual dimension to reality might as well live in flatland. They essentially restrict themselves to a single dimensional world, depriving themselves of the beauty of creation.

Fifth, for those of us who believe Christ rose from the dead, believe He is The Son of God, believe He is the second person of the Trinity, and believe the third person of the Trinity, the Holy Ghost guides the Catholic Church; there is no other choice than to be a Catholic. Since we Catholics believe this, we are duty bound to inform the entire earth about the truth that we have. The cruelest cut would be not sharing the good news of the Gospel with all of Humanity.

Sixth, only Christians believe and teach that God entered the world as both God and man. Yet, it is only the Catholic Church that believes and teaches God is still wholly present to us in the Eucharist. Catholics not only believe that the Bread of Life, the Word of God, entered the world, but we also believe that He remains in the world, and we receive Him body, blood, soul, and divinity in the Eucharist.

Seventh, every person who has ever lived or will live experiences at least one miracle in their lifetime. The miracle of their birth with a soul directly created by God, the fact they have been sent into the world by God, is overlooked as a miracle by many. In addition, God performs miracles according to His plan. They occur in unsuspected places and situations many times and in all places across the globe. Magic and miracles have one aspect which is almost common to both. Both present something which we do not understand. There, any other relationship ends. Magic depends totally on deception and trickery, and once we become aware of how a particular feat was accomplished, we understand all magic is trickery. Miracles, on the other hand, while mysterious will remain so until the return of the King. Miracles are the direct opposite of deception and trickery; they reveal a hidden truth we would not be aware of without them. They also are examples of one of the ways God participates with us in our suffering. Only in Christianity do we have God who joins us in our suffering.

Eighth, from the beginning, Father, Son, and Holy Ghost had a plan for mankind. Human beings were created to be brothers of Christ, and sons of God. The path towards that goal has traversed through our first parents, Noah, Abraham, Isaac, Jacob, Moses, the prophets, and culminated in the Word of God when He came into the world as the infant Jesus on Christmas Day. Since then, the followers of Christ have spread the Gospel throughout the earth. The one and only home of the followers of Jesus on earth, until we enter His kingdom, is the Holy Roman Catholic Church. The evidence is apparent everywhere one looks. Chief among them are the countless acts of kindness, selflessness, generosity, devotion, sacrifice, and love which go unnoticed, unacknowledged, and unpublicized each day of the year. These things are done in the name of Our Lord, Jesus, the Messiah, and the King of Kings, who will return as the conquering hero of all humanity.

The basis for the objection to belief in God and joining the Catholic Church is that there is no empirical evidence to support these claims. One can only adopt such a position if one has a very narrow definition of empirical. A broader definition of empirical includes the spiritual dimension of reality.

Chapter Seven: Be a Catholic / Become a Catholic

From that perspective, which is the correct one, there is an overwhelming amount of empirical proof for God and the Catholic Church. Believe in God and join the Catholic Church.

The Last Word

These are the words of Jesus, Our Lord:

"You have heard that it hath been said, Thou shalt love thy neighbor, and hate thy enemy. But I say to you, Love your enemies: do good to them that hate you: and pray for them that persecute and calumniate you: That you may be the children of your Father who is in heaven, who maketh his sun to rise upon the good, and bad, and raineth upon the just and the unjust. For if you love them that love you, what reward shall you have? Do not also the heathens do this? Be you therefore perfect, as also your heavenly Father is perfect." (Matthew 5:43-48)

This is not easy to practice and live, but it is a command from God, who is the source of all creation. This should be kept in mind when we object to pronouncements coming from the Pope, other members of the clergy, and laity. They are not enemies, and when they are in error we must pray for them. Some may actually turn out to be enemies; we must pray for them as well. I have been critical of Pope Francis in this volume, but I do it with no malice. I offer my objections with deep respect for him and for the office of the papacy. In the parable of the lost sheep, the shepherd goes to find the one sheep that has strayed and is lost. Pope Francis and some of the hierarchy strayed from the faith. When we, the sheep, stray and get lost, we require and expect the shepherd to come and find us and lead us back to the flock. When members of the clergy are lost, we the sheep must find the shepherds and lead them back to the flock. When we see error we should not be silent; we should not sin by omission. I pray that all members of the clergy and laity will follow Our Lord's command and attempt to be perfect. The proven method for Catholics is to pray for all and embrace fasting.

Will this volume convince all men to believe in God, and become Catholic? God came to us in the person of Jesus, and there are still those who refuse to believe. Dostoevsky attributes stubborn disbelief to evil being embedded in every human being. He recognized how great a problem evil is for each individual. His insights are profound. From the Catholic perspective, we would not say evil is an inherent part of human nature, but that the propensity to choose evil is present in each individual. We utilize our free will and choose what we ought not to. Evil has the ability to present itself in variety of seemingly irresistible guises. It is not a partially evil nature, but the fallen nature of man, which makes us all vulnerable. It is in repentance that we are forgiven. In like manner, we are called to forgive.

Today, evil operates by stealth. It is noticeable in modern day liberalism, which has no resemblance to classical liberalism. Liberalism today has embraced the tactics and philosophies of Nazism and Communism, both of which deny God. The tactics have been renamed, dressed up and cloaked in a soft totalitarianism, which operates through societal manipulation, and sophisticated technology. It has leached its way into every aspect of our society. Just as the two Isms mentioned above, liberalism has no tolerance. It is almost impossible to carry on a conversation with the liberally-minded, if one has a differing opinion. The typical reactions are name calling, shouting, accusations, or complete refusal to discuss any issue which does not fit their established narrative. Since secularists believe in no authority outside themselves, they are absolutely sure they have the truth. Any other proposition is beneath their dignity to consider, and any conversation is quickly abrogated. The underlying premise is that Christianity has nothing to offer human civilization. Catholicism is a false superstition; it not only has nothing to offer, it along with Christianity must be eliminated. This is proving to be one of those impediments which are impossible to overcome. In the face of such a juggernaut the only path for Catholics is to live each day following the doctrines of Christ.

It is not only liberalism which is to blame. Due to Original Sin, human nature is frail and easily controlled. There is a need to assess how we measure up to living the message of the Gospel. The place to do just that is in the Catholic Church; it is guided by the magisterium, which is under the protection of the Holy Ghost. The mission of the Holy Roman Catholic Church is to bring all of humanity to Christ, Jesus. He is the only way to the Father, and the way to Jesus is through the Catholic Church.

What if at the end of time, all humanity is gathered for the last judgment, and God tells all of us that if one of us is willing to go out of existence, He will save everyone and everything else He has ever created, even the Devil and his fallen angels. Will anyone step forward to volunteer to be eliminated from existence forever to save all of humanity including the Devil, Hitler, Stalin, the villains who raped wives and daughters and killed sons, and are guilty of innumerable other horrific acts of violence and depravity? Thankfully, no one has to answer or step forward, because Jesus has already accepted that challenge; it was exactly what He faced on the cross; He looked at the face of extinction, and was willing to die for humanity and all of creation. God so loved the world He sent His only Son to save us. We owe all honor and devotion to God. Many men have expressed the idea that God will not condemn us; concerning entering heaven, God will vote for us, the Devil will vote against us, and we will cast the deciding vote. Most frightening is that at that moment, we will have no choice but the self-imposed one to be truthful. Pray to the Father, Son, Holy Ghost, and petition Holy Mary, St. Joseph, and your guardian angel to intercede for you, your family, friends, and for the whole world.

The most profound sound we will each hear in our lifetimes and after we die will be the voice of Christ saying, "Come, ye blessed of my Father, possess you the kingdom prepared for you from the foundation of the world" (Matthew 25:34). Pray and conduct your thoughts and actions in a way of life that will allow you to hear this rather than, "Depart from me, you cursed, into everlasting fire which was prepared for the devil and his angels" (Matthew 25:41).

Terminology

abducent – draw away

acataleptic – incomprehensible

adiaphoristic – theologically indifferent

agathism – all is for the better

allicient – that which attracts

amyctic – irritating

antinomy – contradiction between two authorities

extradictionary – consisting not in words, but in deeds

fabulist- liar

unenvisageable – unimaginable

Note: All biblical quotes are from The Holy Bible, Douay-Rheims Version

www.ingramcontent.com/pod-product-compliance
Lightning Source LLC
Chambersburg PA
CBHW060841050426
42453CB00008B/773